Erato ~ the Muse

Daddy Issue

Wider Perspectives Publishing ¤ 2025 ¤ Hampton Roads, Va.

Cover art by Crickyt J. Expression ~ IG @Crickytseye

Editing by Faith May Griffin ~ IG @the_jupiterwitch

© 2025, Oliver Chauncey-Heine including writing as Erato, the Poet
1st run complete in March 2025
Wider Perspectives Publishing, Hampton Roads, Va.
ISBN 978-1-964531-88-5

In Dedication to my Favorite Poet

Preface

Erato—
I plead you
listen to my heart
hear the beat of my words
set your laurel upon my crown
engrave upon me your roses

Selene—
I plead you
watch me sing
every poor poet knows the moon
and I am no other bastard
I devote my time to thy watchful eye

Hades—
I plead you
feel my cadence
I stand among the dead who
follow you the determined
give my bark a lethal bite

Speaker—
I plead you
say my words with
no more venom than
they desire, no
more love than they deserve

Contents

Preface

(1) Section One. Death
      Ad Nauseam   2

(7) Section Two. Devastation
      Bitter   8
      Newports   9
      Record Player   10
      The Death (of poetry)   11
      Historian   14
      Ribs   17
      Mo(u)rning   19
      Haunted   20
      Melatonin   21
      Hydra   22
      Grief Poem   23
      five stages of grief;   24
      Crystal-clear   26
      Burn-out   27
      Suffering   28
      Dehydration   29
      "Conflict"   31

(33) Section Three. Repercussion

Intent, Means, Plan	34
Developing	35
Chas-him	36
Trolley Problem	37
Crush: to grip tightly	38
Starved	39
My Love	41
Winter	43
Rage	45
Benadryl	47
Last Request	49
Lullaby	51
Incense	54

(57) Section Four. Me

Philautia	58
Nausea	60
Beauty and Bloodshed	61
Potomac Myrtle	63
Henrico Street	66
Red Ribbon	69
Prism	71
Walk Into A Theatre And Yell	73
Woman	75

(79) Section Five. Daddy Issue

1

Death

Ad Nauseam

It's been 4 years since my dad died.
Four years since my world ... died.
I remember too much
     and not enough
Like Mnemosyne was too busy with the Muses
     to check in on me
Like I started drowning in the Styx just enough ...

I remember thinking. Damn
Who's the idiot kid that forgot to get on the bus
today?
       Not mad, just funny—
It's funny, that my middle-school counselor was
the one to pull me off the high-school bus

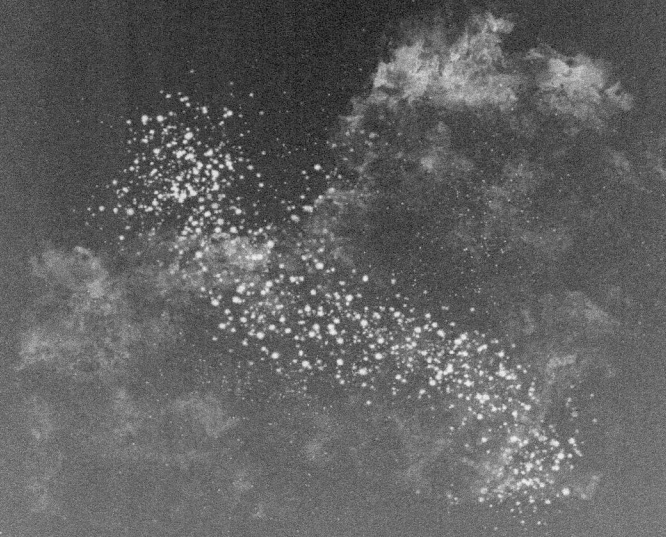

Damn, I'm the fucking idiot kid

I was sure I was in trouble
I must have asked her 6 times what I did.
"Nothin,"
Like the start of a sentence
she never got to finish

I remember 3 words.
3 words like
I love you
I miss you
I am sorry

Baby, Daddy's Dead

Baby, I am 6 years old
    and my daddy's filing a police report
    on the preteen boy that kissed me

Baby, I am 12 years old
    and he is cheering me on as I struggle
    to survive

Baby, I am 14
    and manic
Baby, I am 15
    and hate him
Baby, I am 16
    and love him
Baby, I am 17
    and he's dead.

Daddy,

   where are my goodnight kisses ?

Daddy,

   where is my orange juice ?

Daddy,

   I am sick again

Daddy,

   hold my hand

Daddy,

   squeeze my hand like you used to

Daddy,

   I cannot breathe with you on the floor

Dead.

    10:33 AM every day I flinch

Dead.

    Can't drive without seeing you

    in the rearview

Dead.
Dead.
Dead.

    On the ground bones broken

Bleeding
Bleeding
Bleeding
Dead.

Devastation 2

Bitter

You may find solace
in the similarities of the aspects
between a dead man
and a living one,

but I do not share
the grief of a microphone
and I do not wish to be subjected to it

Newports

I look outside
and notice that it has finally
stopped raining.

Someone is smoking
on the balcony. I
think of you,

I didn't think
it would ever stop
raining.

Record Player

I'm rewriting
history
Recording over the sound of your voice,
what a lonely endeavor
to walk the street alone.
No shutter clicks. No smoke.
Just the scratch of the needle
and a song I don't know

The Death (of poetry)

They say
The death of poetry is bloody
bleeding out too fast on the asphalt.
They say it is hemophilia.
Words too thin to stick to a page,
Whispers too quiet to catch the mic.
They say the death of poetry is the death
Of a forty-eight year old man.
No one knows
The death of poetry is
      Frown lines
      Therapy
      Tears in pages
      Years worth reading about

Daddy Issue

No one knows the death of poetry is

  Greying hair

  Hazel eyes

No one knows it is a father

Poetry would be fifty-two today

Poetry would be at my wedding,

my graduation.

Poetry is a father

bleeding out

ribs broken.

Poetry is explicit

It's death cannot be censored.

The death of poetry?

The death of poetry is a

"jack-of-all-trades" a

"moped accident" a

"loss of a legend"

The death of poetry is "life-
threatening injuries"
The death of poetry is "Opinionated"
The death of poetry is -
"THIS ARTICLE IS ONLY AVAILABLE
TO SUBSCRIBERS"

The death of poetry was a father
always running late.

http://www.pilotonline.com/2020/02/27/ghent-staple-jeff-
hewitt-dies-in-moped-crash-on-colley-avenue/

Historian

I try not to think about it.
Death, that is.

Death that creeps its way into the house

Death that catches your voice with its teeth

Death that crawls into your bones to hide

Death that cries its agony 'til it's everywhere

     flooded.

I place it in a drawer
with everything else too demanding
my pocket watch that needs new batteries,
last week's medication,

every journal that pours through my identities,
the volume of my words,
the swelling of my ignorance,
everything too demanding.
Object permanence has never been my
         strong suit
I think that
by crushing the skull filled with everything
         that could be
into the drawer in the back of my own that
                  I hope it'll leave.
That I don't have to do anything to retrieve
         its potential.

But that is not how grief works.
It takes
It demands
It never asks.

So, when the beetles that catalog the books
in my mind snag their legs over the edges of
memories I don't want scribed –
... ...
You can burn all the books you want
ignite the feather quills and
melt the pens.
But the fumes are just another memory to hide

Grief spills eventually
whether we write it,
hide its ink well,
or burn it.

Ribs

I was eating dinner,
barbecue ribs,
when it hit me. I had to
go. Dinner half-eaten. Did Your Ribs Break?
Did they shatter on impact?
Into little shards.   Thrown from your body.
I haven't had meat on the bone since.
... ...
... ...
I've seen the photos
of the accident.
The bike you worked on so lovingly
lay like rock candy
strewn against the pavement as if

I had dropped it in the kitchen.
Sticky.
Crunchy.
Useless.

Mo(u)rning

I tried to do anything
but lay in bed all day.

On days where I do nothing but think of you,
I can't look our family in the eyes
without my chest caving in.

I don't remember this part well,
but then again,
I don't remember the first year either.

Then from day to night, there I was,
curled in my safe fuzzy blanket,
with a candle burning on my desk,
and you in my palm.

Haunted

I think
my house is haunted

Not with evil spirits
or even gentle ones

But with
the ghost of our memories

Melatonin

I think that death is a dream.
Not in the philosophical sense—
only the gods can see what waits us—
but in the sense that the first one pulls you under
and you only get to wake up when it's time for
your own

Hydra

It is a snake,
that curls in my stomach.
It writhes in my intestines,
climbs my esophagus and constricts my throat.
I choke on him.

Choke on the venom he spits through my
digestive tract
I feel his scales mesh with my skin
transforming my shoulders to snakeskin

I feel him slide up my spine
fusing the vertebrae.

He constructs my being
feeding on the mistrust stored in my bones.

Grief Poem

I wish I could cradle
my beating heart
in the palms of my hands to
thank it;
but
my hands would fumble,

                                              spill it onto the pavement
for the sparrows to pick at
I wish it weren't so
      that I could just   hold   myself   together.
But I can't.
the glue holding my bones is melting
and all I can do

                                                    is turn out the
                                                      lights.

Five stages of grief

He told me I could give someone the world
with a poem,
"Love poems are dangerous," he said,
"powerful; be wary of who you pour your ink into."
But the only one I write to now is him.

The clock hands mock us, tick. tick. tick. Almost
feels like a charlatan's martyrdom
the way the hourglass shattered, piercing us
through and through and through.
He told me I could give someone the world with a
poem.

Maybe I want the world. To hell with this system
full of venom,
I am tired of society
I am tired of writing this poem.
But the only one I write to now is him.

I hate it. Poetry. A brand of searing words,
holding me for ransom
filling my heart with tar, every rhythm, every
rhyme, everything that made me unglue.

He told me I could give someone the world
with a poem. But the only one I write to now
is him.

Crystal-clear

I couldn't, at first, feel the rage.
It sat outside my door, the rage
held itself from me like a lover to sea. Rage
wasn't just in my pastime. Rage
saw my bedclothes and left me for sadness.

But I can see you clearly now. The rage
is here. Pounding on my bedroom door. Rage
flows through bones and smothers in my sleep.
Rage
gets drunk with me in the morning. I'm
done mourning
you. There is only rage.

Burn-out

I screamed so loud as a kid,
but I am older now
my throat is hoarse, and my body broken;
complicit in my own privilege,
fighting my own demons

I fight when I can

but it is so far and between

that I can speak louder than a whimper

Suffering

I sob   and I scream
I do not know how to suffer any other way
as if the nausea,   the speechlessness,
is the only thing
     Validating my grief
As if the only way to feel is with my

                        every
                        thing.

If it does not torment me deeply –
Do I even feel?
Do I love?
I sob and I sob and I scream
'til the candle is a puddle on the floor
along with my very being,
black cherry wax, mixed with salty tears

Dehydration

I – am running on empty –
running with worn out shoes –
and an empty water bottle –

I poured it out ages ago –
Desperate to water a dying plant –
Desperate to scream a little louder –
Desperate to say something –
Desperate to be something –

My father told me I'd run out of words –

My father told me to scream a little quieter –

I was giving him a headache –

Daddy Issue

Good. My head aches –

with the pain of thousands –

My head aches –

and I am running on empty –

I am thirsty –

But I am running –

"Conflict"

I don't know how to make this poem
Impersonal;
how can I separate myself from the words?
We are glued,
wires through our rib cages
wires through our meaning and our echo
the children are dying;
the lovers are dying
and I am just a wordsmith,
desperately trying.

I am bleeding out; when I see his face

when I see the blade, carving him from me.

I can only cry; I can only watch

as he is severed from my ribcage

cast from me like God is punishing him for
my sins

punishing him for my complacency.

Complacency. Is that what we call a war with no
end?

Have you considered the lone soldier
the lone poet, artist, muse
echoing their prayers on the page
bullet-holes scattering their thoughts
like the bullet holes scattering the people?

There is no simile here; just war.

3
Repercussion

Intent, Means, Plan

Killing myself is
too much hassle
It's easier to just get
my life together
I think

Developing

The ghost of you
is transposed over me
like a photograph.

Our fingers overlap
and I sit, in the darkroom,
red lights casting over my
grimace, willing our hands to touch.

Chas-him

I taste him
on the tip of my tongue sometimes
Like cherries
and rum
like grenadine and mint.

I've fallen in love
with the frog in your throat
how you slot against my hips
how you feel in my hand
I see you in how the trees shed their leaves
how a flower wilts
how i rot
with-
out you.

Trolley Problem

I don't know why I'm at the lever
and tied to the tracks
and I don't know whether
you're the trolley
or the ropes holding me down.

Daddy Issue

Crush: to grip tightly

I always write about love
like it's a disease
an affliction
an arrow through my heart
lacerating and
bleeding me dry. Aching.

I'm

coughing up flowers
and crying stardust

and falling for you

bleeding out, and falling for you

Starved

God doesn't tell you when you're starving.

You get no pangs of hunger. Starvation

is gradual. Creeping. Smothering.

It takes you rib by rib – swallowing you

whole until you are just bone. 'Til the tips

of your fingers are pressed to your carotid

and you are screaming. 'Til they are swallowed

into the hole in your chest, the great cavern,

collapsing heart -

God doesn't tell you when you're starving.

But when you taste for the first time. and it
consumes you faster than you can swallow.
When the bruises bloom on your skin and the
pain brings you to life?
That is when you know.
That's when the starving
quiets. When it stops.
The first breath you take,
satiated. Screams
of your starvation.

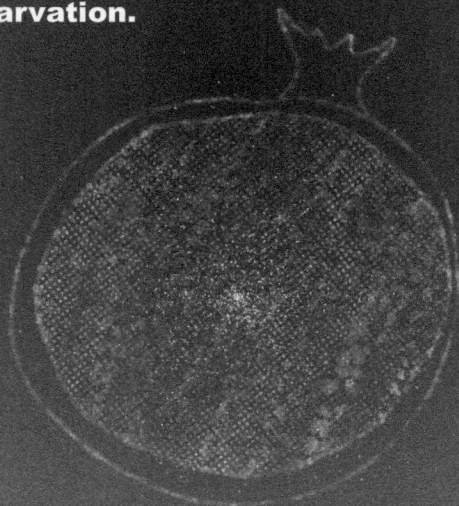

My Love

My love comes from my shoulders
rolling and tearing,
it stretches
it reaches out
pulling itself from the socket to reach you
pulling itself forward

My love comes from my hips
with a crack they pop back into place
I tentatively move to see if you reciprocate intent
the searing pain doesn't give me an answer

My love comes from my knees
they overextend into party tricks
"See what my love can do"
anything to distract
from actually loving you

Winter

Burn me with ambrosia

Crack my ribcage
like the pomegranates blessed Kore tasted,
damning us with frostbite.

Watch my lungs compress
choking the bitter air
that you leave in your wake.
Watch my heart stutter and squirm

No longer protected by its iron cage
No longer protected from the harsh winds
No longer protected from your ice-cold gaze.

Rip me open, throw me to Tartarus
cast me from our mortal plane
leave me to pick up the pieces.

Sweet Iambe, with her wicked words
jest with me,
my darling; lest the winter frost swallow us
whole.

Rage

I didn't want to write about you yesterday
the blood was too fresh on my hands—
two years of scrubbing hasn't
closed the wound.
Even in not writing-
I wrote about you
funny, how that works.
Actualizing the pain.
I've thrown myself
unbidden
into Styx.

It seeps through
and covers me with its currents.
Rage gets drunk with me in the morning.

Can't escape vi'lent
kisses and bruised knuckles. Its vigilant
eyes consume me in its wake.
Hunger. Star –

vation of the highest quality. Bar
on the floor kinda rage. Bar in fucking
Hell kinda rage. Bar in the recesses
of my fucking mind and soul kinda rage.

Benadryl

I am healing from you.

Slowly.

I am picking up the shards of bone you

ripped through me.

Tending to my bruises. Tending to my scars.

Sewing up the pieces of my heart that lie

shattered amongst the other things in life I

let be abused.

You consume me.

Stuck in this nightmare state- the

Hat Man laughs at my misery.

I am stuck, immobile, dreaming

of how you love me.

Do you love me?

Last Request

You haven't asked me why I left
I've rehearsed it a million times
The words chalk in my mouth
Powder burns on my lips

I've thought about you crying
You raging
You loving me hating me begging me
I hope it hurt you. As much as it hurt me

'Cause maybe the water in my lungs
Would taste sweeter
If you were choking, too

Daddy Issue

If you spit and cried and screamed
I'd tell you that you put a gun in my mouth
Safety off, demanding I pull the trigger
Kill myself to love you
Bite back the bullets
Or breathe freely but barely breathe

Do I choke on blood or tears tonight?
I slit my wrists the night you did it
Five minutes before it happened
Preemptive salvation for my broken heart

Fate weaves many strands- and you
Picked the one that hung me from the trees
You swore to never prick me with your thorns
and branches
And yet I bleed

And oh, how I bleed
Crimson petals dotting paper i's like a promise

i miss you;
i love you;
i hope that's enough;
i know it's not.

Lullaby

Burnt chips of your love fill my nostrils
like cypress bark pressed between my fingertips
roughly cutting into my delicate skin
I cry fire, but I'm the one who set you ablaze
This forest is the same I kissed you in
and yet
I can't help but watch it go up in flames

Your words to me, bittersweet
truth or lies dressed in a vinegar glaze
choking me with its violet haze

The smoke burns my eyes
that's the reason I'll keep to my grave
never that you made me feel this way

Petal by petal
He loves me
He loves you
He loves me
He loves you
He left me
He chose you

And here I am burning
still fighting the flames to kiss you
my blood stains the earth red
but white roses never were your thing

The fire licks through the grass
ashing white and just for a moment
I wish it would take me with it

It washes over me
like you did
burns off the scar tissue
and continues on its way

Oh how raw I am

like Orpheus, I do not know my own tragedy

Where is the irony

Where is the chorus

Where is my resolution

How can I promise not to look back when you are
so close to me

If I had known

loving you would kill me

Would I let you split my heart in three

Would I let you spill acid on my arms

Would I let you soil my brain with lies

If I had known
would I still love you?

Incense

My lover has teeth aimed
at my jugular
My carotid dances in their grasp and
for a moment
I plead for silence

The buzz of the lights
the hum of the radio
My lover sinks their jaws into my skin
tearing into the flesh like jello

I bruise like an apple, crisp, split
the blood viscous and sweet

My lover has their teeth aimed
at my very lifeblood
sickly blue and bitter to
the morning sun
burning me
to a crisp

dried lavender and
rose petals
fuzzy on my tongue
heavy against my veins
oil seeping into the grooves
of my fingerprints
altering the standing of
who we are
hive-mind of petals
curling into my windpipe
blooming on my tongue

I'm self destructive
by my own design
curbing my ambitions
freezing my inhibitions

If I never fly
I'll never fall
I'll never skin my knees on the pavement.

Philautia

after Rowan Perez, @rid.inkskinned

'Where does love come from?'
my philosophy teacher asks.
He means the drive. The virtue.
But all I can think of is "red blood. black ink."
        "i am terrified (jugular vein)" -
I feel it in my sternum

Love comes from just right of my spine
it wraps itself up, across my ribs
it flows through the veins in my arms
breaks through the skin of my wrists
snakes over my palm before it
swallows my fingertips

Always embedded in the print of
who I am

Daddy Issue

Nausea

I get motion sickness

each phrase of my life
every line of poetry
hurtling
nonconsentually spilling from my lips
bleeding out from my lungs
nausea from the words swirling in my stomach
kicking to get out
to vomit onto the page
to stain my fingertips in blood and
bruise my lips
in their urgency

Beauty and Bloodshed

I am a child of Aphrodite,
for like her,
my life began with something severed.
Seafoam and doves
pool water and pigeons

They cast me from their place of war
and designated me fragile.
Fragile.   Fragile like porcelain
too pretty to touch
Reserved for special occasions only
        life is a special occasion only
I crack on my own will
solder myself in gold and

display myself for my own pleasure
As much as I live, oh do I rage.
Oh do I rage
Leading wars like I depend on the bloodlust
Pride is my sin and it looks an awful lot like
Wrath
So watch as I pull myself from the ocean
pearly and glimmering
radiant
I am a child of Aphrodite
Beauty and Bloodlust are in my veins

Potomac Myrtle

Pink flowers crumble in my hand,
I've always loved the softness against my
fingerprints.
    I climbed that tree once.
    To get away from her prying hands.
    To get a little closer to the sky.
    I didn't have the words then.
    Didn't have the hindsight.
Made my home in the neighborhood trees.
Made my home with the ants and paper-bark.
Made my home in the branches of a crape myrtle.

Potomac, they call it.

Patawomeck.

I don't want to think of my brother right now
    This isn't his poem
    This isn't a bathroom stall
    I'm not writing in sharpie.
    Not writing in blood

Who am I outside those trees?
Outside the grass I killed as I ran away?
Outside the tree I had my first kiss against?
The bark we stripped in elementary school to
write against?

I lost my identity a while ago.
Lost it in the ocean currents pulling me under
    Lost it in the sand
Is my identity my memories? Is it my words?
Is it the grass welting my skin?

If it is my words,
it is every poem I've written in the sand
every time I whispered into the wind
every pleading prayer I've sung to the moon.

The rose bushes lining my lawn
The hydrangeas climbing my stairs

The willow the oak the cherry blossom

The ocean has always washed my sins
I just didn't realize
It had washed away the rest of me.

Henrico Street

When I was a kid

there was a little girl who

would pick purple flowers

and run her teeth over the stems.

They tasted bitter. Sour. Home.

There was a little boy that would climb

the orange tree in the backyard.

He'd pick them by hand

wincing at the citrus that stung his bramble-cuts.

That orange tree rotted years ago.

The brambles choked it

to death. Tore apart his roots.

Tore apart the necklace he'd strung.

Blackberries feed on tears and blood,

don't you know?

She stopped eating stems that day.

Planted mint instead. Let it cover her ankles.

Let it climb the porch where

her little white cat lay

buried. Let it fight the thorns

let it cover that rotted stump.

I'm much older now.

Burned the backyard with gasoline

dug up the roots. Planted moss instead.

A blanket to cover my memories. To cover

the little girl; the little boy;

give them something to sleep on.

To cover oxygen-starved nights

hiding in the ivy-stained shed

hiding from the creeping vines

the blotched marks of its poison

marking my ankles my thighs my breasts

marking my heart

in its demanding gaze

I burned that backyard with gasoline.

Wonder if that's why

nothing grows anymore -

why the moss crumbled away -

the soil is poisoned.

no wasps build their nests

against my window,

the dandelions refuse to grow,

refuse to lend me their seeds.

said i'm rotted inside

said those blackberry brambles choked me too.

Red Ribbon

I walk the line and
sometimes it consumes me
sometimes I tie it around my wrists to calm
my thrashing
sometimes I tie it around my throat and cry
It will never be enough to kill me
to undo the crimes committed in my name
to rid myself of the blood I've spilled
the remains I've buried
Justice does not come with a neat little bow
of pavement
You have to hunt for that shit

You have to write, you have to breathe,
you have to drown and learn that the water does
not sting as much as it used to

Prism

When God made me,
She asked if I wanted to be loved
or good. I looked at her
blinded by the grief I hadn't yet had
and told her I wanted to be loved.
I could choose to be good. Good was on reserve
inside me but love, love?
Love happened to me; I couldn't make love,
couldn't build butterflies couldn't build
blush marks or the sick feeling you get
when you realize you're up too high.

Daddy Issue

God looked at me and smiled

So when I realized I was queer I cried

You told me I'd be loved, God

You told me they'd love me

So when I realized I was queer I cried

I didn't know love

could come in different shades

could see that the rainbow hue was

still a damned color

even if it was a color I could swallow

I could starve from

Walk Into A Theatre And Yell

I wish
it were a coat
or a blanket.
A weight I could shrug

Step away from,
just to breath

In an undimmed breath of water
something to drown it
The thoughts and
doubt anything could heal it

Scoffed fabric burns holes in skin,
hair that ribbons. Curling black from the smoke

Would the match be enough
A Molotov
to burn the silver engravings

Places that should never have been mapped
misfiring on pathways that should never be
walked
messages that should have been left unread
But this dirt road is far too familiar
mud cakes at the edges
of the page even now
tarring perfect words making
ink blur at its corners making
the book heavier, shaking.

If it were a coat
I wouldn't be so cold
as to set myself on fire

Woman

I am a woman, like the
raindrops sliding down my face
I am a woman,
in the way of lightning
I am feminine, like purple poison
I am endless
I am a woman, like sight reading
through notes on a page for the strings to sing
I am staccato
I am the baseline, but never the melody
I am a woman, the same way I am a man
in half shades and muted tones
closer to nature than humanity
closer to shadows than sunshine
I am endless

Daddy Issue

Rusted gears in a wind-up music box that stutters
a desperate song for someone no longer around to
hear it

I am a woman
like sand melting into glass
like dough rising
like the caterpillar crystallizing
I am a woman
for as long as I need to be
for as long as you need me to be

These mirrors are one-way glass, my love
and you see your own reflection when you look at
me but I see straight through you
Straight through the frosted edges of your words
and one day I will break this mirror and cut you
with it
and when your blood stains my cheeks red

maybe you will understand

I am woman like crimson red

like cheshire blue, like poison purple

I am a woman in every way I am not
I am a woman
and a man
I am everything in between and
everything that is not
I am
I just am

Daddy Issue

Daddy Issue

There is no reply to
the prayers I whisper –
the prayers I scream –

I ... am selfish,
insomuch as every poem is about me
because every poem is about you –
Selfish in the way I hold your memory
in every street corner every pen stroke
– selfish ...

Like you're still here. Like
you're just grabbing some coffee ... some smokes
...
some thing – any thing – that means you'll be back

but, men, kill men, every, damn, day

my poem cannot stop you from bleeding out
my poem does not even know it is just
a poem

I hold no hate to the man
        (and I assume that it is a man)
that killed you.
He did not know any better
        (we never do)

So, I take my Lamictal every night
the Abilify sits somewhere in the corner of
my room
from – a "fit" of "rage" – that maybe I
heard your voice amongst those in my brain

my brain... quiets. under the pills – shadows
dance at the edge of my vision ... ...
... ...
I thought it was you
My pills make you go away
they make my blood red, not gold

You see – my blood ... wants me dead (like you)
Wants me to (gut myself) tear the knife (like you
tore on concrete) to save the lizards (crawling)

in my stomach.

It wants me to carve this poem into my lungs
My blood – – –
my blood wants me to kill myself
(hanging from the rafters) I had to take away
my blood's shoelaces (razor blade | kitchen knife)
I had to ration its cough syrup
(1 sheep, 2 sheep, 3)
We've tried CBT   ABA   DBT   EKG – My blood
doesn't want to do today's journal.
– – – but it will
It's on the way [my blood] is not my own
(like my last name, it is a gift, like the guitar picks
in my backpack)

I don't like the blues – don't like jazz – don't
like the way your guitar catches in my throat
don't like the ... lullabies
T he way   my   ey es   d r   if   t —
                              (to the side of the road)
to the possum – that crossed too late —
          (torn open on asphalt)
I don't like the blues

I find – they put me – too harshly – to sleep
I wake up, covered in blood like
every night since you left
Checked all my old scars to make sure
they hadn't closed up yet
(but it hadn't been me)
(had only been you)
(bleeding through the
                    seam of my shirt)
I had only been me
standing on your stage...
Holy ground... Sacred ground...
Hole-filled ground – scared to ground
myself against the cold cold blood in January
my bleeding pen sacrilegious paper
sifting through trashy poetry
Looking for you — always — looking for you —
in my words.
am I cloth . bone . my father's . dna . his
little poet boy — po'try boy
(begging   to go home)
    (to a life   of absence)

Somebody makes a joke
about a car crash and I see you
bloodied   I see you
bloodied   my ribs ache

are they bruised like you were?
are they broken like you were?
Somebody makes a joke
am I broken   like you were?
Broken like the trees you shattered with
the aluminum baseball bat that sits by my head,
it's dented —   (like you were?)
It's seen its years of grief
after all
the skye wept the day you left
What bastard son am I?

See ... I
am half of you.
        half the man you'll ever be
        half the words you'd ever speak
        half the picture frame ...
        half ... the ... poem
have the guts to tell you

I changed my last name.

I couldn't handle the weight
of you on my chest
Couldn't bare your sins on collateral
with my own—   your son is dead
I am   all   that remains
his words   are all   that remains

You see,
my father and I view poetry
differently

Poetry has never been my bastard lover
never a graveyard
        never knife wounds
an overdose
Poetry   is medicinal

A salve to lessen the scars
A suture to stop us from bleeding
out onto the page
Poetry   is salvation

my father and I
view po'try
differently,
to say the least.
Perhaps, that is because,
He
views poetry as some   thing,
and I
view po'try, as
him.

www.ingramcontent.com/pod-product-compliance
Lightning Source LLC
Chambersburg PA
CBHW031145090426
42738CB00008B/1234